BEER TASTING JOURNAL

THIS JOURNAL BELONGS TO

Beer Tasting Journal

Date ....

Beer Name ....

Style .... Brewery ....

Price .... Place Tasted ....

Serving Type

- ☐ Bottle ☐ Can ☐ Growler
- ☐ Draft   ☐ Cask ☐ ....

Appearance	Taste	Smell
Mouthfeel	Drinkability	Overall Impression

Notes

....
....
....

Rating ☆ ☆ ☆ ☆

Beer Tasting Journal

Date ....

Beer Name ....

Style .... Brewery ....

Price .... Place Tasted ....

Serving Type

- ☐ Bottle
- ☐ Can
- ☐ Growler
- ☐ Draft
- ☐ Cask
- ☐ ....

Appearance	Taste	Smell

Mouthfeel	Drinkability	Overall Impression

Notes

....
....
....

Rating ☆ ☆ ☆ ☆ ☆

Beer Tasting Journal

Date ....

Beer Name ....

Style .... Brewery ....

Price .... Place Tasted ....

Serving Type

- ☐ Bottle ☐ Can ☐ Growler
- ☐ Draft   ☐ Cask ☐ ....

Appearance	Taste	Smell
Mouthfeel	Drinkability	Overall Impression

Notes

....
....
....

Rating ☆ ☆ ☆ ☆ ☆

Beer Tasting Journal

Date ....

Beer Name ....

Style .... Brewery ....

Price .... Place Tasted ....

Serving Type

☐ Bottle ☐ Can ☐ Growler
☐ Draft ☐ Cask ☐ ....

| Appearance | Taste | Smell |

| Mouthfeel | Drinkability | Overall Impression |

Notes

....
....
....

Rating ☆ ☆ ☆ ☆ ☆

Beer Tasting Journal

Date ....

Beer Name ....

Style .... Brewery ....

Price .... Place Tasted ....

Serving Type

☐ Bottle ☐ Can ☐ Growler
☐ Draft ☐ Cask ☐ ....

Appearance	Taste	Smell
Mouthfeel	Drinkability	Overall Impression

Notes

....
....
....

Rating ☆ ☆ ☆ ☆ ☆

Beer Tasting Journal

Date ....

Beer Name ....

Style .... Brewery ....

Price .... Place Tasted ....

Serving Type

☐ Bottle ☐ Can ☐ Growler
☐ Draft   ☐ Cask ☐ ....

Appearance	Taste	Smell
Mouthfeel	Drinkability	Overall Impression

Notes

....
....
....

Rating ☆ ☆ ☆ ☆ ☆

Beer Tasting Journal

Date ....

Beer Name ....

Style .... Brewery ....

Price .... Place Tasted ....

Serving Type

- ☐ Bottle   ☐ Can   ☐ Growler
- ☐ Draft   ☐ Cask   ☐ ....

Appearance	Taste	Smell
Mouthfeel	Drinkability	Overall Impression

Notes

....
....
....

Rating ☆ ☆ ☆ ☆ ☆

Beer Tasting Journal

Date ....

Beer Name ....

Style .... Brewery ....

Price .... Place Tasted ....

Serving Type

- ☐ Bottle   ☐ Can   ☐ Growler
- ☐ Draft   ☐ Cask   ☐ ....

Appearance	Taste	Smell
Mouthfeel	Drinkability	Overall Impression

Notes

....
....
....

Rating ☆ ☆ ☆ ☆ ☆

Beer Tasting Journal

Date ....

Beer Name ....

Style .... Brewery ....

Price .... Place Tasted ....

Serving Type

- ☐ Bottle
- ☐ Can
- ☐ Growler
- ☐ Draft
- ☐ Cask
- ☐ ....

Appearance	Taste	Smell
Mouthfeel	Drinkability	Overall Impression

Notes

....
....
....

Rating ☆ ☆ ☆ ☆ ☆

Beer Tasting Journal

Date ....

Beer Name ....

Style .... Brewery ....

Price .... Place Tasted ....

Serving Type

- ☐ Bottle
- ☐ Can
- ☐ Growler
- ☐ Draft
- ☐ Cask
- ☐ ....

Appearance	Taste	Smell

Mouthfeel	Drinkability	Overall Impression

Notes

....
....
....

Rating ⭐ ⭐ ⭐ ⭐ ⭐

Beer Tasting Journal

Date ....

Beer Name ....

Style .... Brewery ....

Price .... Place Tasted ....

Serving Type

- ☐ Bottle   ☐ Can   ☐ Growler
- ☐ Draft   ☐ Cask ☐ ....

Appearance	Taste	Smell
Mouthfeel	Drinkability	Overall Impression

Notes

....

....

....

Rating ☆ ☆ ☆ ☆ ☆

Beer Tasting Journal

Date ....

Beer Name ....

Style .... Brewery ....

Price .... Place Tasted ....

Serving Type

- ☐ Bottle ☐ Can ☐ Growler
- ☐ Draft ☐ Cask ☐ ....

Appearance	Taste	Smell
Mouthfeel	Drinkability	Overall Impression

Notes

....
....
....

Rating ☆ ☆ ☆ ☆ ☆

Beer Tasting Journal

Date ....

Beer Name ....

Style .... Brewery ....

Price .... Place Tasted ....

Serving Type

☐ Bottle   ☐ Can   ☐ Growler
☐ Draft   ☐ Cask ☐ ....

Appearance	Taste	Smell
Mouthfeel	Drinkability	Overall Impression

Notes

....
....
....

Rating ★ ★ ★ ★ ★

Beer Tasting Journal

Date ....

Beer Name ....

Style .... Brewery ....

Price .... Place Tasted ....

Serving Type

- ☐ Bottle ☐ Can ☐ Growler
- ☐ Draft ☐ Cask ☐ ....

Appearance	Taste	Smell

Mouthfeel	Drinkability	Overall Impression

Notes

....
....
....

Rating ☆ ☆ ☆ ☆ ☆

Beer Tasting Journal

Date ....

Beer Name ....

Style .... Brewery ....

Price .... Place Tasted ....

Serving Type

- ☐ Bottle ☐ Can ☐ Growler
- ☐ Draft   ☐ Cask ☐ ....

Appearance	Taste	Smell

Mouthfeel	Drinkability	Overall Impression

Notes

....

....

....

Rating ☆ ☆ ☆ ☆ ☆

Beer Tasting Journal

Date ....

Beer Name ....

Style .... Brewery ....

Price .... Place Tasted ....

Serving Type

☐ Bottle ☐ Can ☐ Growler
☐ Draft   ☐ Cask ☐ ....

Appearance	Taste	Smell
Mouthfeel	Drinkability	Overall Impression

Notes

....
....
....

Rating ⭐ ⭐ ⭐ ⭐ ⭐

Beer Tasting Journal

Date ....

Beer Name ....

Style .... Brewery ....

Price .... Place Tasted ....

Serving Type

☐ Bottle ☐ Can ☐ Growler
☐ Draft ☐ Cask ☐ ....

Appearance	Taste	Smell
Mouthfeel	Drinkability	Overall Impression

Notes

....
....
....

Rating ★ ★ ★ ★ ★

Beer Tasting Journal

Date ....

Beer Name ....

Style .... Brewery ....

Price .... Place Tasted ....

Serving Type

☐ Bottle ☐ Can ☐ Growler
☐ Draft ☐ Cask ☐ ....

Appearance	Taste	Smell
Mouthfeel	Drinkability	Overall Impression

Notes

....
....
....

Rating ☆ ☆ ☆ ☆ ☆

Beer Tasting Journal

Date ....

Beer Name ....

Style .... Brewery ....

Price .... Place Tasted ....

Serving Type

- ☐ Bottle
- ☐ Can
- ☐ Growler
- ☐ Draft
- ☐ Cask
- ☐ ....

Appearance	Taste	Smell
Mouthfeel	Drinkability	Overall Impression

Notes

....
....
....

Rating ★ ★ ★ ★

Beer Tasting Journal

Date ....

Beer Name ....

Style .... Brewery ....

Price .... Place Tasted ....

Serving Type

☐ Bottle ☐ Can ☐ Growler
☐ Draft ☐ Cask ☐ ....

Appearance	Taste	Smell
Mouthfeel	Drinkability	Overall Impression

Notes

....
....
....

Rating ☆ ☆ ☆ ☆ ☆

Beer Tasting Journal

Date ....

Beer Name ....

Style .... Brewery ....

Price .... Place Tasted ....

Serving Type

- ☐ Bottle   ☐ Can   ☐ Growler
- ☐ Draft   ☐ Cask   ☐ ....

Appearance	Taste	Smell
Mouthfeel	Drinkability	Overall Impression

Notes

....
....
....

Rating ☆ ☆ ☆ ☆ ☆

Beer Tasting Journal

Date ....

Beer Name ....

Style .... Brewery ....

Price .... Place Tasted ....

Serving Type

- ☐ Bottle
- ☐ Can
- ☐ Growler
- ☐ Draft
- ☐ Cask
- ☐ ....

Appearance	Taste	Smell

Mouthfeel	Drinkability	Overall Impression

Notes

....
....
....

Rating ☆ ☆ ☆ ☆ ☆

Beer Tasting Journal

Date ....

Beer Name ....

Style .... Brewery ....

Price .... Place Tasted ....

Serving Type

- ☐ Bottle   ☐ Can   ☐ Growler
- ☐ Draft   ☐ Cask   ☐ ....

Appearance	Taste	Smell
Mouthfeel	Drinkability	Overall Impression

Notes

....
....
....

Rating ☆ ☆ ☆ ☆ ☆

Beer Tasting Journal

Date ....

Beer Name ....

Style .... Brewery ....

Price .... Place Tasted ....

Serving Type

☐ Bottle ☐ Can ☐ Growler
☐ Draft   ☐ Cask ☐ ....

Appearance	Taste	Smell
Mouthfeel	Drinkability	Overall Impression

Notes

....
....
....

Rating ☆ ☆ ☆ ☆ ☆

Beer Tasting Journal

Date

Beer Name ....

Style .... Brewery ....

Price .... Place Tasted ....

Serving Type

- ☐ Bottle ☐ Can ☐ Growler
- ☐ Draft   ☐ Cask ☐ ....

Appearance	Taste	Smell
Mouthfeel	Drinkability	Overall Impression

Notes

....
....
....

Rating ☆ ☆ ☆ ☆

Beer Tasting Journal

Date ....

Beer Name ....

Style .... Brewery ....

Price .... Place Tasted ....

Serving Type

☐ Bottle ☐ Can ☐ Growler
☐ Draft ☐ Cask ☐ ....

Appearance	Taste	Smell
Mouthfeel	Drinkability	Overall Impression

Notes

....
....
....

Rating ☆ ☆ ☆ ☆ ☆

Beer Tasting Journal

Date ....

Beer Name ....

Style .... Brewery ....

Price .... Place Tasted ....

Serving Type

- ☐ Bottle ☐ Can ☐ Growler
- ☐ Draft   ☐ Cask ☐ ....

Appearance	Taste	Smell

Mouthfeel	Drinkability	Overall Impression

Notes

....

....

....

Rating ☆ ☆ ☆ ☆ ☆

Beer Tasting Journal

Date ....

Beer Name ....

Style .... Brewery ....

Price .... Place Tasted ....

Serving Type

☐ Bottle ☐ Can ☐ Growler
☐ Draft ☐ Cask ☐ ....

Appearance	Taste	Smell
Mouthfeel	Drinkability	Overall Impression

Notes

....
....
....

Rating ☆ ☆ ☆ ☆ ☆

Beer Tasting Journal

Date ....

Beer Name ....

Style .... Brewery ....

Price .... Place Tasted ....

Serving Type

☐ Bottle   ☐ Can   ☐ Growler
☐ Draft   ☐ Cask ☐ ....

Appearance	Taste	Smell
Mouthfeel	Drinkability	Overall Impression

Notes

....
....
....

Rating ☆ ☆ ☆ ☆ ☆

Beer Tasting Journal

Date ....

Beer Name ....

Style .... Brewery ....

Price .... Place Tasted ....

Serving Type

- ☐ Bottle ☐ Can ☐ Growler
- ☐ Draft ☐ Cask ☐ ....

Appearance	Taste	Smell
Mouthfeel	Drinkability	Overall Impression

Notes

....
....
....

Rating ☆ ☆ ☆ ☆ ☆

Beer Tasting Journal

Date ....

Beer Name ....

Style .... Brewery ....

Price .... Place Tasted ....

Serving Type

- ☐ Bottle
- ☐ Can
- ☐ Growler
- ☐ Draft
- ☐ Cask
- ☐ ....

Appearance	Taste	Smell
Mouthfeel	Drinkability	Overall Impression

Notes

....
....
....

Rating ☆ ☆ ☆ ☆

Beer Tasting Journal

Date ....

Beer Name ....

Style .... Brewery ....

Price .... Place Tasted ....

Serving Type

☐ Bottle ☐ Can ☐ Growler
☐ Draft   ☐ Cask ☐ ....

Appearance	Taste	Smell

Mouthfeel	Drinkability	Overall Impression

Notes

....
....
....

Rating ☆ ☆ ☆ ☆ ☆

Beer Tasting Journal

Date ....

Beer Name ....

Style .... Brewery ....

Price .... Place Tasted ....

Serving Type

- ☐ Bottle   ☐ Can   ☐ Growler
- ☐ Draft   ☐ Cask ☐ ....

Appearance	Taste	Smell
Mouthfeel	Drinkability	Overall Impression

Notes

....
....
....

Rating ★ ★ ★ ★ ★

Beer Tasting Journal

Date ....

Beer Name ....

Style .... Brewery ....

Price .... Place Tasted ....

Serving Type

☐ Bottle ☐ Can ☐ Growler
☐ Draft   ☐ Cask ☐ ....

Appearance	Taste	Smell
Mouthfeel	Drinkability	Overall Impression

Notes

....
....
....

Rating ☆ ☆ ☆ ☆ ☆

Beer Tasting Journal

Date ....

Beer Name ....

Style .... Brewery ....

Price .... Place Tasted ....

Serving Type

- ☐ Bottle   ☐ Can   ☐ Growler
- ☐ Draft   ☐ Cask   ☐ ....

Appearance	Taste	Smell

Mouthfeel	Drinkability	Overall Impression

Notes

....

....

....

Rating ☆ ☆ ☆ ☆ ☆

Beer Tasting Journal

Date ....

Beer Name ....

Style .... Brewery ....

Price .... Place Tasted ....

Serving Type

- ☐ Bottle ☐ Can ☐ Growler
- ☐ Draft ☐ Cask ☐ ....

Appearance	Taste	Smell
Mouthfeel	Drinkability	Overall Impression

Notes

....
....
....

Rating ☆ ☆ ☆ ☆ ☆

Beer Tasting Journal

Date ....

Beer Name ....

Style .... Brewery ....

Price .... Place Tasted ....

Serving Type

- ☐ Bottle
- ☐ Can
- ☐ Growler
- ☐ Draft
- ☐ Cask
- ☐ ....

Appearance	Taste	Smell
Mouthfeel	Drinkability	Overall Impression

Notes

....
....
....

Rating ★ ★ ★ ★ ★

Beer Tasting Journal

Date ....

Beer Name ....

Style .... Brewery ....

Price .... Place Tasted ....

Serving Type

☐ Bottle   ☐ Can   ☐ Growler
☐ Draft   ☐ Cask   ☐ ....

Appearance	Taste	Smell
Mouthfeel	Drinkability	Overall Impression

Notes

....
....
....

Rating ☆ ☆ ☆ ☆

Beer Tasting Journal

Date ....

Beer Name ....

Style .... Brewery ....

Price .... Place Tasted ....

Serving Type

- ☐ Bottle
- ☐ Can
- ☐ Growler
- ☐ Draft
- ☐ Cask
- ☐ ....

Appearance	Taste	Smell

Mouthfeel	Drinkability	Overall Impression

Notes

....
....
....

Rating ☆ ☆ ☆ ☆

Beer Tasting Journal

Date ....

Beer Name ....

Style .... Brewery ....

Price .... Place Tasted ....

Serving Type

- ☐ Bottle
- ☐ Can
- ☐ Growler
- ☐ Draft
- ☐ Cask
- ☐ ....

Appearance	Taste	Smell
Mouthfeel	Drinkability	Overall Impression

Notes

....
....
....

Rating ☆ ☆ ☆ ☆ ☆

Beer Tasting Journal

Date ....

Beer Name ....

Style .... Brewery ....

Price .... Place Tasted ....

Serving Type

- ☐ Bottle   ☐ Can   ☐ Growler
- ☐ Draft   ☐ Cask   ☐ ....

Appearance	Taste	Smell
Mouthfeel	Drinkability	Overall Impression

Notes

....
....
....

Rating ☆ ☆ ☆ ☆ ☆

Beer Tasting Journal

Date ....

Beer Name ....

Style .... Brewery ....

Price .... Place Tasted ....

Serving Type

- ☐ Bottle ☐ Can ☐ Growler
- ☐ Draft ☐ Cask ☐ ....

Appearance	Taste	Smell
Mouthfeel	Drinkability	Overall Impression

Notes

....
....
....

Rating ★ ★ ★ ★ ★

Beer Tasting Journal

Date ....

Beer Name ....

Style .... Brewery ....

Price .... Place Tasted ....

Serving Type

☐ Bottle ☐ Can ☐ Growler
☐ Draft ☐ Cask ☐ ....

Appearance	Taste	Smell

Mouthfeel	Drinkability	Overall Impression

Notes

....
....
....

Rating ☆ ☆ ☆ ☆ ☆

Beer Tasting Journal

Date ....

Beer Name ....

Style .... Brewery ....

Price .... Place Tasted ....

Serving Type

- ☐ Bottle ☐ Can ☐ Growler
- ☐ Draft ☐ Cask ☐ ....

Appearance	Taste	Smell
Mouthfeel	Drinkability	Overall Impression

Notes

....
....
....

Rating ⭐ ⭐ ⭐ ⭐ ⭐

Beer Tasting Journal

Date ....

Beer Name ....

Style .... Brewery ....

Price .... Place Tasted ....

Serving Type

- ☐ Bottle
- ☐ Can
- ☐ Growler
- ☐ Draft
- ☐ Cask
- ☐ ....

Appearance	Taste	Smell
Mouthfeel	Drinkability	Overall Impression

Notes

....
....
....

Rating ☆ ☆ ☆ ☆ ☆

Beer Tasting Journal

Date ....

Beer Name ....

Style .... Brewery ....

Price .... Place Tasted ....

Serving Type

- ☐ Bottle ☐ Can ☐ Growler
- ☐ Draft ☐ Cask ☐ ....

Appearance	Taste	Smell
Mouthfeel	Drinkability	Overall Impression

Notes

....
....
....

Rating ☆ ☆ ☆ ☆ ☆

Beer Tasting Journal

Date ....

Beer Name ....

Style .... Brewery ....

Price .... Place Tasted ....

Serving Type

- ☐ Bottle
- ☐ Can
- ☐ Growler
- ☐ Draft
- ☐ Cask
- ☐ ....

Appearance	Taste	Smell
Mouthfeel	Drinkability	Overall Impression

Notes

....
....
....

Rating ★ ★ ★ ★ ★

Beer Tasting Journal

Date ....

Beer Name ....

Style .... Brewery ....

Price .... Place Tasted ....

Serving Type

☐ Bottle ☐ Can   ☐ Growler
☐ Draft   ☐ Cask ☐ ....

Appearance	Taste	Smell
Mouthfeel	Drinkability	Overall Impression

Notes

....
....
....

Rating ☆ ☆ ☆ ☆ ☆

Beer Tasting Journal

Date ....

Beer Name ....

Style .... Brewery ....

Price .... Place Tasted ....

Serving Type

☐ Bottle   ☐ Can   ☐ Growler
☐ Draft   ☐ Cask   ☐ ....

Appearance	Taste	Smell

Mouthfeel	Drinkability	Overall Impression

Notes

....
....
....

Rating ☆ ☆ ☆ ☆ ☆

Beer Tasting Journal

Date ....

Beer Name ....

Style .... Brewery ....

Price .... Place Tasted ....

Serving Type

☐ Bottle   ☐ Can   ☐ Growler
☐ Draft   ☐ Cask   ☐ ....

Appearance	Taste	Smell
Mouthfeel	Drinkability	Overall Impression

Notes

....
....
....

Rating ⭐ ⭐ ⭐ ⭐ ⭐

Beer Tasting Journal

Date ....

Beer Name ....

Style .... Brewery ....

Price .... Place Tasted ....

Serving Type

- ☐ Bottle
- ☐ Can
- ☐ Growler
- ☐ Draft
- ☐ Cask
- ☐ ....

Appearance	Taste	Smell
Mouthfeel	Drinkability	Overall Impression

Notes

....
....
....

Rating ☆ ☆ ☆ ☆ ☆

Beer Tasting Journal

Date ....

Beer Name ....

Style .... Brewery ....

Price .... Place Tasted ....

Serving Type

☐ Bottle ☐ Can ☐ Growler
☐ Draft ☐ Cask ☐ ....

Appearance	Taste	Smell
Mouthfeel	Drinkability	Overall Impression

Notes

....
....
....

Rating ☆ ☆ ☆ ☆ ☆

Beer Tasting Journal

Date

Beer Name ....

Style .... Brewery ....

Price .... Place Tasted ....

Serving Type

☐ Bottle ☐ Can ☐ Growler
☐ Draft   ☐ Cask ☐ ....

Appearance	Taste	Smell
Mouthfeel	Drinkability	Overall Impression

Notes

....
....
....

Rating ★ ★ ★ ★

Beer Tasting Journal

Date ....

Beer Name ....

Style .... Brewery ....

Price .... Place Tasted ....

Serving Type

☐ Bottle ☐ Can ☐ Growler
☐ Draft   ☐ Cask ☐ ....

Appearance	Taste	Smell
Mouthfeel	Drinkability	Overall Impression

Notes

....
....
....

Rating ★ ★ ★ ★ ★

Beer Tasting Journal

Date ....

Beer Name ....

Style .... Brewery ....

Price .... Place Tasted ....

Serving Type

- ☐ Bottle
- ☐ Can
- ☐ Growler
- ☐ Draft
- ☐ Cask
- ☐ ....

Appearance	Taste	Smell
Mouthfeel	Drinkability	Overall Impression

Notes

....
....
....

Rating ★ ★ ★ ★ ★

Beer Tasting Journal

Date ....

Beer Name ....

Style .... Brewery ....

Price .... Place Tasted ....

Serving Type

- ☐ Bottle   ☐ Can   ☐ Growler
- ☐ Draft   ☐ Cask   ☐ ....

Appearance	Taste	Smell
Mouthfeel	Drinkability	Overall Impression

Notes

....
....
....

Rating ★ ★ ★ ★ ★

Beer Tasting Journal

Date ....

Beer Name ....

Style .... Brewery ....

Price .... Place Tasted ....

Serving Type

- ☐ Bottle
- ☐ Can
- ☐ Growler
- ☐ Draft
- ☐ Cask
- ☐ ....

Appearance	Taste	Smell

Mouthfeel	Drinkability	Overall Impression

Notes

....
....
....

Rating ☆ ☆ ☆ ☆ ☆

Beer Tasting Journal

Date ....

Beer Name ....

Style .... Brewery ....

Price .... Place Tasted ....

Serving Type

- ☐ Bottle
- ☐ Can
- ☐ Growler
- ☐ Draft
- ☐ Cask
- ☐ ....

Appearance	Taste	Smell
Mouthfeel	Drinkability	Overall Impression

Notes

....
....
....

Rating ☆ ☆ ☆ ☆ ☆

Beer Tasting Journal

Date ....

Beer Name ....

Style .... Brewery ....

Price .... Place Tasted ....

Serving Type

- [ ] Bottle
- [ ] Can
- [ ] Growler
- [ ] Draft
- [ ] Cask
- [ ] ....

Appearance	Taste	Smell
Mouthfeel	Drinkability	Overall Impression

Notes

....
....
....

Rating ☆ ☆ ☆ ☆

Beer Tasting Journal

Date ....

Beer Name ....

Style .... Brewery ....

Price .... Place Tasted ....

Serving Type

- ☐ Bottle   ☐ Can   ☐ Growler
- ☐ Draft   ☐ Cask ☐ ....

Appearance	Taste	Smell

Mouthfeel	Drinkability	Overall Impression

Notes

....
....
....

Rating   ☆ ☆ ☆ ☆ ☆

Beer Tasting Journal

Date ....

Beer Name ....

Style .... Brewery ....

Price .... Place Tasted ....

Serving Type

- ☐ Bottle ☐ Can ☐ Growler
- ☐ Draft   ☐ Cask ☐ ....

Appearance	Taste	Smell

Mouthfeel	Drinkability	Overall Impression

Notes

....

....

....

Rating ☆ ☆ ☆ ☆ ☆

Beer Tasting Journal

Date ....

Beer Name ....

Style .... Brewery ....

Price .... Place Tasted ....

Serving Type

☐ Bottle ☐ Can ☐ Growler
☐ Draft   ☐ Cask ☐ ....

Appearance	Taste	Smell
Mouthfeel	Drinkability	Overall Impression

Notes

....
....
....

Rating ★ ★ ★ ★ ★

Beer Tasting Journal

Date ....

Beer Name ....

Style .... Brewery ....

Price .... Place Tasted ....

Serving Type

- ☐ Bottle ☐ Can ☐ Growler
- ☐ Draft ☐ Cask ☐ ....

Appearance	Taste	Smell
Mouthfeel	Drinkability	Overall Impression

Notes

....
....
....

Rating ★ ★ ★ ★ ★

Beer Tasting Journal

Date

Beer Name ....

Style .... Brewery ....

Price .... Place Tasted ....

Serving Type

- ☐ Bottle ☐ Can ☐ Growler
- ☐ Draft ☐ Cask ☐ ....

Appearance	Taste	Smell

Mouthfeel	Drinkability	Overall Impression

Notes

....
....
....

Rating ★ ★ ★ ★ ★

Beer Tasting Journal

Date ....

Beer Name ....

Style .... Brewery ....

Price .... Place Tasted ....

Serving Type

☐ Bottle ☐ Can ☐ Growler
☐ Draft ☐ Cask ☐ ....

Appearance	Taste	Smell
Mouthfeel	Drinkability	Overall Impression

Notes

....
....
....

Rating ☆ ☆ ☆ ☆

Beer Tasting Journal

Date ....

Beer Name ....

Style .... Brewery ....

Price .... Place Tasted ....

Serving Type

- ☐ Bottle
- ☐ Can
- ☐ Growler
- ☐ Draft
- ☐ Cask
- ☐ ....

Appearance	Taste	Smell

Mouthfeel	Drinkability	Overall Impression

Notes

....

....

....

Rating ☆ ☆ ☆ ☆ ☆

Beer Tasting Journal

Date ....

Beer Name ....

Style .... Brewery ....

Price .... Place Tasted ....

Serving Type

- ☐ Bottle
- ☐ Can
- ☐ Growler
- ☐ Draft
- ☐ Cask
- ☐ ....

Appearance	Taste	Smell

Mouthfeel	Drinkability	Overall Impression

Notes

....
....
....

Rating ★ ★ ★ ★ ★

Beer Tasting Journal

Date ....

Beer Name ....

Style .... Brewery ....

Price .... Place Tasted ....

Serving Type

- ☐ Bottle   ☐ Can   ☐ Growler
- ☐ Draft   ☐ Cask   ☐ ....

Appearance	Taste	Smell
Mouthfeel	Drinkability	Overall Impression

Notes

....
....
....

Rating ★ ★ ★ ★ ★

Beer Tasting Journal

Date ....

Beer Name ....

Style .... Brewery ....

Price .... Place Tasted ....

Serving Type

- ☐ Bottle ☐ Can ☐ Growler
- ☐ Draft ☐ Cask ☐ ....

Appearance	Taste	Smell
Mouthfeel	Drinkability	Overall Impression

Notes

....
....
....

Rating ☆ ☆ ☆ ☆ ☆

Beer Tasting Journal

Date ....

Beer Name ....

Style .... Brewery ....

Price .... Place Tasted ....

Serving Type

☐ Bottle ☐ Can ☐ Growler
☐ Draft   ☐ Cask ☐ ....

Appearance	Taste	Smell
Mouthfeel	Drinkability	Overall Impression

Notes

....
....
....

Rating ⭐ ⭐ ⭐ ⭐ ⭐

Beer Tasting Journal

Date ....

Beer Name ....

Style .... Brewery ....

Price .... Place Tasted ....

Serving Type

☐ Bottle ☐ Can ☐ Growler
☐ Draft ☐ Cask ☐ ....

Appearance	Taste	Smell
Mouthfeel	Drinkability	Overall Impression

Notes

....
....
....

Rating ☆ ☆ ☆ ☆ ☆

Beer Tasting Journal

Date ....

Beer Name ....

Style .... Brewery ....

Price .... Place Tasted ....

Serving Type

☐ Bottle ☐ Can ☐ Growler
☐ Draft ☐ Cask ☐ ....

Appearance	Taste	Smell
Mouthfeel	Drinkability	Overall Impression

Notes

....
....
....

Rating ☆ ☆ ☆ ☆ ☆

Beer Tasting Journal

Date ....

Beer Name ....

Style .... Brewery ....

Price .... Place Tasted ....

Serving Type

- ☐ Bottle   ☐ Can   ☐ Growler
- ☐ Draft   ☐ Cask   ☐ ....

Appearance	Taste	Smell

Mouthfeel	Drinkability	Overall Impression

Notes

....
....
....

Rating ☆ ☆ ☆ ☆ ☆

Beer Tasting Journal

Date ....

Beer Name ....

Style .... Brewery ....

Price .... Place Tasted ....

Serving Type

- ☐ Bottle
- ☐ Can
- ☐ Growler
- ☐ Draft
- ☐ Cask
- ☐ ....

Appearance	Taste	Smell
Mouthfeel	Drinkability	Overall Impression

Notes

....
....
....

Rating ★ ★ ★ ★ ★

Beer Tasting Journal

Date ....

Beer Name ....

Style .... Brewery ....

Price .... Place Tasted ....

Serving Type

☐ Bottle ☐ Can ☐ Growler
☐ Draft ☐ Cask ☐ ....

Appearance	Taste	Smell

Mouthfeel	Drinkability	Overall Impression

Notes

....
....
....

Rating ☆ ☆ ☆ ☆ ☆

Beer Tasting Journal

Date ....

Beer Name ....

Style .... Brewery ....

Price .... Place Tasted ....

Serving Type

☐ Bottle   ☐ Can   ☐ Growler
☐ Draft   ☐ Cask   ☐ ....

Appearance	Taste	Smell
Mouthfeel	Drinkability	Overall Impression

Notes

....
....
....

Rating ☆ ☆ ☆ ☆ ☆

Beer Tasting Journal

Date ....

Beer Name ....

Style .... Brewery ....

Price .... Place Tasted ....

Serving Type

- ☐ Bottle ☐ Can ☐ Growler
- ☐ Draft ☐ Cask ☐ ....

Appearance	Taste	Smell
Mouthfeel	Drinkability	Overall Impression

Notes

....
....
....

Rating ☆ ☆ ☆ ☆ ☆

Beer Tasting Journal

Date ....

Beer Name ....

Style .... Brewery ....

Price .... Place Tasted ....

Serving Type

- ☐ Bottle ☐ Can ☐ Growler
- ☐ Draft ☐ Cask ☐ ....

Appearance	Taste	Smell
Mouthfeel	Drinkability	Overall Impression

Notes

....
....
....

Rating ★ ★ ★ ★ ★

Beer Tasting Journal

Date ....

Beer Name ....

Style .... Brewery ....

Price .... Place Tasted ....

Serving Type

- ☐ Bottle ☐ Can ☐ Growler
- ☐ Draft ☐ Cask ☐ ....

Appearance	Taste	Smell
Mouthfeel	Drinkability	Overall Impression

Notes

....
....
....

Rating ☆ ☆ ☆ ☆ ☆

Beer Tasting Journal

Date ....

Beer Name ....

Style .... Brewery ....

Price .... Place Tasted ....

Serving Type

- ☐ Bottle
- ☐ Can
- ☐ Growler
- ☐ Draft
- ☐ Cask
- ☐ ....

Appearance	Taste	Smell
Mouthfeel	Drinkability	Overall Impression

Notes

....
....
....

Rating ☆ ☆ ☆ ☆ ☆

Beer Tasting Journal

Date ....

Beer Name ....

Style .... Brewery ....

Price .... Place Tasted ....

Serving Type

- ☐ Bottle
- ☐ Can
- ☐ Growler
- ☐ Draft
- ☐ Cask
- ☐ ....

Appearance	Taste	Smell
Mouthfeel	Drinkability	Overall Impression

Notes

....
....
....

Rating ☆ ☆ ☆ ☆ ☆

Beer Tasting Journal

Date ....

Beer Name ....

Style .... Brewery ....

Price .... Place Tasted ....

Serving Type

- ☐ Bottle
- ☐ Can
- ☐ Growler
- ☐ Draft
- ☐ Cask
- ☐ ....

Appearance	Taste	Smell

Mouthfeel	Drinkability	Overall Impression

Notes

....
....
....

Rating ⭐ ⭐ ⭐ ⭐ ⭐

Beer Tasting Journal

Date ....

Beer Name ....

Style .... Brewery ....

Price .... Place Tasted ....

Serving Type

- ☐ Bottle
- ☐ Can
- ☐ Growler
- ☐ Draft
- ☐ Cask
- ☐ ....

Appearance	Taste	Smell

Mouthfeel	Drinkability	Overall Impression

Notes

....
....
....

Rating ☆ ☆ ☆ ☆ ☆

Beer Tasting Journal

Date ....

Beer Name ....

Style .... Brewery ....

Price .... Place Tasted ....

Serving Type

- ☐ Bottle ☐ Can ☐ Growler
- ☐ Draft ☐ Cask ☐ ....

Appearance	Taste	Smell
Mouthfeel	Drinkability	Overall Impression

Notes

....
....
....

Rating ☆ ☆ ☆ ☆ ☆

Beer Tasting Journal

Date ....

Beer Name ....

Style .... Brewery ....

Price .... Place Tasted ....

Serving Type

- ☐ Bottle
- ☐ Can
- ☐ Growler
- ☐ Draft
- ☐ Cask
- ☐ ....

Appearance	Taste	Smell
Mouthfeel	Drinkability	Overall Impression

Notes

....
....
....

Rating ★ ★ ★ ★ ★

Beer Tasting Journal

Date ....

Beer Name ....

Style .... Brewery ....

Price .... Place Tasted ....

Serving Type

☐ Bottle ☐ Can ☐ Growler
☐ Draft   ☐ Cask ☐ ....

Appearance	Taste	Smell

Mouthfeel	Drinkability	Overall Impression

Notes

....
....
....

Rating ☆ ☆ ☆ ☆ ☆

Beer Tasting Journal

Date ....

Beer Name ....

Style .... Brewery ....

Price .... Place Tasted ....

Serving Type

- ☐ Bottle ☐ Can ☐ Growler
- ☐ Draft   ☐ Cask ☐ ....

Appearance	Taste	Smell
Mouthfeel	Drinkability	Overall Impression

Notes

....
....
....

Rating ☆ ☆ ☆ ☆ ☆

Beer Tasting Journal

Date ....

Beer Name ....

Style .... Brewery ....

Price .... Place Tasted ....

Serving Type

- ☐ Bottle ☐ Can ☐ Growler
- ☐ Draft ☐ Cask ☐ ....

Appearance	Taste	Smell
Mouthfeel	Drinkability	Overall Impression

Notes

....

....

....

Rating ☆ ☆ ☆ ☆ ☆

Beer Tasting Journal

Date ....

Beer Name ....

Style .... Brewery ....

Price .... Place Tasted ....

Serving Type

☐ Bottle   ☐ Can   ☐ Growler
☐ Draft   ☐ Cask ☐ ....

Appearance	Taste	Smell

Mouthfeel	Drinkability	Overall Impression

Notes

....
....
....

Rating ☆ ☆ ☆ ☆ ☆

Beer Tasting Journal

Date ....

Beer Name ....

Style .... Brewery ....

Price .... Place Tasted ....

Serving Type

- ☐ Bottle ☐ Can ☐ Growler
- ☐ Draft   ☐ Cask ☐ ....

Appearance	Taste	Smell

Mouthfeel	Drinkability	Overall Impression

Notes

....
....
....

Rating ☆ ☆ ☆ ☆ ☆

Beer Tasting Journal

Date ....

Beer Name ....

Style .... Brewery ....

Price .... Place Tasted ....

Serving Type

- ☐ Bottle ☐ Can ☐ Growler
- ☐ Draft ☐ Cask ☐ ....

Appearance	Taste	Smell
Mouthfeel	Drinkability	Overall Impression

Notes

....

....

....

Rating ★ ★ ★ ★ ★

Beer Tasting Journal

Date ....

Beer Name ....

Style .... Brewery ....

Price .... Place Tasted ....

Serving Type

☐ Bottle ☐ Can ☐ Growler
☐ Draft ☐ Cask ☐ ....

Appearance	Taste	Smell
Mouthfeel	Drinkability	Overall Impression

Notes

....

....

....

Rating ☆ ☆ ☆ ☆ ☆

Beer Tasting Journal

Date ....

Beer Name ....

Style .... Brewery ....

Price .... Place Tasted ....

Serving Type

- ☐ Bottle ☐ Can ☐ Growler
- ☐ Draft   ☐ Cask ☐ ....

Appearance	Taste	Smell

Mouthfeel	Drinkability	Overall Impression

Notes

....
....
....

Rating ★ ★ ★ ★ ★

Beer Tasting Journal

Date ....

Beer Name ....

Style .... Brewery ....

Price .... Place Tasted ....

Serving Type

- ☐ Bottle
- ☐ Can
- ☐ Growler
- ☐ Draft
- ☐ Cask
- ☐ ....

Appearance	Taste	Smell

Mouthfeel	Drinkability	Overall Impression

Notes

....
....
....

Rating ☆ ☆ ☆ ☆ ☆

Beer Tasting Journal

Date ....

Beer Name ....

Style .... Brewery ....

Price .... Place Tasted ....

Serving Type

☐ Bottle   ☐ Can   ☐ Growler
☐ Draft   ☐ Cask   ☐ ....

Appearance	Taste	Smell
Mouthfeel	Drinkability	Overall Impression

Notes

....
....
....

Rating ☆ ☆ ☆ ☆ ☆

Beer Tasting Journal

Date ....

Beer Name ....

Style .... Brewery ....

Price .... Place Tasted ....

Serving Type

- ☐ Bottle ☐ Can ☐ Growler
- ☐ Draft   ☐ Cask ☐ ....

Appearance	Taste	Smell
Mouthfeel	Drinkability	Overall Impression

Notes

....
....
....

Rating ★ ★ ★ ★ ★

Beer Tasting Journal

Date ....

Beer Name ....

Style .... Brewery ....

Price .... Place Tasted ....

Serving Type

☐ Bottle   ☐ Can   ☐ Growler
☐ Draft   ☐ Cask   ☐ ....

Appearance	Taste	Smell

Mouthfeel	Drinkability	Overall Impression

Notes

....
....
....

Rating ☆ ☆ ☆ ☆ ☆

Beer Tasting Journal

Date ....

Beer Name ....

Style .... Brewery ....

Price .... Place Tasted ....

Serving Type

- ☐ Bottle ☐ Can ☐ Growler
- ☐ Draft ☐ Cask ☐ ....

Appearance	Taste	Smell
Mouthfeel	Drinkability	Overall Impression

Notes

....
....
....

Rating ☆ ☆ ☆ ☆ ☆

Beer Tasting Journal

Date ....

Beer Name ....

Style .... Brewery ....

Price .... Place Tasted ....

Serving Type

☐ Bottle ☐ Can ☐ Growler
☐ Draft   ☐ Cask ☐ ....

Appearance	Taste	Smell
Mouthfeel	Drinkability	Overall Impression

Notes

....
....
....

Rating ☆ ☆ ☆ ☆ ☆

Beer Tasting Journal

Date ....

Beer Name ....

Style .... Brewery ....

Price .... Place Tasted ....

Serving Type

☐ Bottle ☐ Can ☐ Growler
☐ Draft ☐ Cask ☐ ....

Appearance	Taste	Smell
Mouthfeel	Drinkability	Overall Impression

Notes

....
....
....

Rating ☆ ☆ ☆ ☆ ☆

Beer Tasting Journal

Date ....

Beer Name ....

Style .... Brewery ....

Price .... Place Tasted ....

Serving Type

- ☐ Bottle
- ☐ Can
- ☐ Growler
- ☐ Draft
- ☐ Cask
- ☐ ....

Appearance	Taste	Smell
Mouthfeel	Drinkability	Overall Impression

Notes

....
....
....

Rating ☆ ☆ ☆ ☆ ☆

Beer Tasting Journal

Date ....

Beer Name ....

Style .... Brewery ....

Price .... Place Tasted ....

Serving Type

- ☐ Bottle
- ☐ Can
- ☐ Growler
- ☐ Draft
- ☐ Cask
- ☐ ....

Appearance	Taste	Smell
Mouthfeel	Drinkability	Overall Impression

Notes

....
....
....

Rating ☆ ☆ ☆ ☆ ☆

Beer Tasting Journal

Date ....

Beer Name ....

Style .... Brewery ....

Price .... Place Tasted ....

Serving Type

- ☐ Bottle   ☐ Can   ☐ Growler
- ☐ Draft   ☐ Cask   ☐ ....

Appearance	Taste	Smell

Mouthfeel	Drinkability	Overall Impression

Notes

....
....
....

Rating ☆ ☆ ☆ ☆ ☆

Beer Tasting Journal

Date ....

Beer Name ....

Style .... Brewery ....

Price .... Place Tasted ....

Serving Type

☐ Bottle ☐ Can ☐ Growler
☐ Draft ☐ Cask ☐ ....

Appearance	Taste	Smell
Mouthfeel	Drinkability	Overall Impression

Notes

....
....
....

Rating ☆ ☆ ☆ ☆ ☆

Beer Tasting Journal

Date ....

Beer Name ....

Style .... Brewery ....

Price .... Place Tasted ....

Serving Type

- ☐ Bottle ☐ Can ☐ Growler
- ☐ Draft   ☐ Cask ☐ ....

Appearance	Taste	Smell
Mouthfeel	Drinkability	Overall Impression

Notes

....
....
....

Rating ⭐ ⭐ ⭐ ⭐ ⭐

Beer Tasting Journal

Date ....

Beer Name ....

Style .... Brewery ....

Price .... Place Tasted ....

Serving Type

- ☐ Bottle
- ☐ Can
- ☐ Growler
- ☐ Draft
- ☐ Cask
- ☐ ....

Appearance	Taste	Smell
Mouthfeel	Drinkability	Overall Impression

Notes

....
....
....

Rating ⭐ ⭐ ⭐ ⭐ ⭐

Beer Tasting Journal

Date ....

Beer Name ....

Style .... Brewery ....

Price .... Place Tasted ....

Serving Type

☐ Bottle ☐ Can ☐ Growler
☐ Draft ☐ Cask ☐ ....

Appearance	Taste	Smell
Mouthfeel	Drinkability	Overall Impression

Notes

....
....
....

Rating ☆ ☆ ☆ ☆ ☆

Beer Tasting Journal

Date ....

Beer Name ....

Style .... Brewery ....

Price .... Place Tasted ....

Serving Type

- ☐ Bottle
- ☐ Can
- ☐ Growler
- ☐ Draft
- ☐ Cask
- ☐ ....

Appearance	Taste	Smell
Mouthfeel	Drinkability	Overall Impression

Notes

....
....
....

Rating ☆ ☆ ☆ ☆ ☆

Beer Tasting Journal

Date ....

Beer Name ....

Style .... Brewery ....

Price .... Place Tasted ....

Serving Type

- ☐ Bottle ☐ Can ☐ Growler
- ☐ Draft ☐ Cask ☐ ....

Appearance	Taste	Smell
Mouthfeel	Drinkability	Overall Impression

Notes

....
....
....

Rating ☆ ☆ ☆ ☆ ☆

Beer Tasting Journal

Date ....

Beer Name ....

Style .... Brewery ....

Price .... Place Tasted ....

Serving Type

- ☐ Bottle   ☐ Can   ☐ Growler
- ☐ Draft   ☐ Cask   ☐ ....

Appearance	Taste	Smell
Mouthfeel	Drinkability	Overall Impression

Notes

....
....
....

Rating ★ ★ ★ ★ ★

Beer Tasting Journal

Date ....

Beer Name ....

Style .... Brewery ....

Price .... Place Tasted ....

Serving Type

☐ Bottle ☐ Can ☐ Growler
☐ Draft ☐ Cask ☐ ....

Appearance	Taste	Smell
Mouthfeel	Drinkability	Overall Impression

Notes

....
....
....

Rating ☆ ☆ ☆ ☆ ☆

Beer Tasting Journal

Date ....

Beer Name ....

Style .... Brewery ....

Price .... Place Tasted ....

Serving Type

☐ Bottle ☐ Can ☐ Growler
☐ Draft ☐ Cask ☐ ....

Appearance	Taste	Smell
Mouthfeel	Drinkability	Overall Impression

Notes

....
....
....

Rating ★ ★ ★ ★ ★

Beer Tasting Journal

Date ....

Beer Name ....

Style .... Brewery ....

Price .... Place Tasted ....

Serving Type

☐ Bottle ☐ Can ☐ Growler
☐ Draft   ☐ Cask ☐ ....

| Appearance | Taste | Smell |
| Mouthfeel | Drinkability | Overall Impression |

Notes

....
....
....

Rating ☆ ☆ ☆ ☆ ☆

Beer Tasting Journal

Date ....

Beer Name ....

Style .... Brewery ....

Price .... Place Tasted ....

Serving Type

- ☐ Bottle ☐ Can ☐ Growler
- ☐ Draft   ☐ Cask ☐ ....

Appearance	Taste	Smell
Mouthfeel	Drinkability	Overall Impression

Notes

....
....
....

Rating ⭐ ⭐ ⭐ ⭐ ⭐

Beer Tasting Journal

Date ....

Beer Name ....

Style .... Brewery ....

Price .... Place Tasted ....

Serving Type

- ☐ Bottle ☐ Can ☐ Growler
- ☐ Draft ☐ Cask ☐ ....

Appearance	Taste	Smell
Mouthfeel	Drinkability	Overall Impression

Notes

....
....
....

Rating ★ ★ ★ ★ ★

Beer Tasting Journal

Date ....

Beer Name ....

Style .... Brewery ....

Price .... Place Tasted ....

Serving Type

- ☐ Bottle
- ☐ Can
- ☐ Growler
- ☐ Draft
- ☐ Cask
- ☐ ....

Appearance	Taste	Smell

Mouthfeel	Drinkability	Overall Impression

Notes

....
....
....

Rating ☆ ☆ ☆ ☆ ☆

Beer Tasting Journal

Date ....

Beer Name ....

Style .... Brewery ....

Price .... Place Tasted ....

Serving Type

- ☐ Bottle
- ☐ Can
- ☐ Growler
- ☐ Draft
- ☐ Cask
- ☐ ....

Appearance	Taste	Smell
Mouthfeel	Drinkability	Overall Impression

Notes

....
....
....

Rating ☆ ☆ ☆ ☆ ☆

Beer Tasting Journal

Date ....

Beer Name ....

Style .... Brewery ....

Price .... Place Tasted ....

Serving Type

- ☐ Bottle ☐ Can ☐ Growler
- ☐ Draft ☐ Cask ☐ ....

Appearance	Taste	Smell
Mouthfeel	Drinkability	Overall Impression

Notes

....
....
....

Rating ☆ ☆ ☆ ☆

Beer Tasting Journal

Date ....

Beer Name ....

Style .... Brewery ....

Price .... Place Tasted ....

Serving Type

☐ Bottle   ☐ Can   ☐ Growler
☐ Draft   ☐ Cask ☐ ....

Appearance	Taste	Smell

Mouthfeel	Drinkability	Overall Impression

Notes

....
....
....

Rating ☆ ☆ ☆ ☆ ☆

www.ingramcontent.com/pod-product-compliance
Lightning Source LLC
LaVergne TN
LVHW081538070526
838199LV00056B/3704